CURRENT SCIENCE®

The Exterminator
Wiping Out the World's Most Infectious Diseases

By Kristi Lew

Reading Adviser: Cecilia Minden-Cupp, Ph.D., Literacy Consultant
Content Adviser: Elaine Vernetti, M.D., M.P.H.

Gareth Stevens
Publishing

Please visit our web site at **www.garethstevens.com**.
For a free color catalog describing Gareth Stevens Publishing's list of
high-quality books, call 1-800-542-2595 (USA) or 1-800-387-3178 (Canada).
Gareth Stevens Publishing's fax: 1-877-542-2596

Library of Congress Cataloging-in-Publication Data

Lew, Kristi.
    The exterminator : wiping out the world's most infectious diseases / by Kristi Lew ; reading consultant, Cecilia Minden-Cupp ; medical adviser, Elaine Vernetti.
       p. cm. — (Current science)
    Includes bibliographical references and index.
    ISBN-10: 1-4339-2061-1   ISBN-13: 978-1-4339-2061-5 (lib. bdg.)
    1. Medical microbiology—Juvenile literature. 2. Communicable diseases—Juvenile literature.
3. Microorganisms—Juvenile literature. 4. Immunity—Juvenile literature. I. Title.
  QR46.L65   2010
  616.9—dc22
                                                                                                                    2009002276

This edition first published in 2010 by
Gareth Stevens Publishing
A Weekly Reader® Company
1 Reader's Digest Road
Pleasantville, NY 10570-7000 USA

Copyright © 2010 by Gareth Stevens, Inc.

Current Science™ is a trademark of Weekly Reader Corporation. Used under license.

Gareth Stevens Executive Managing Editor: Lisa M. Herrington
Gareth Stevens Senior Editor: Barbara Bakowski
Gareth Stevens Cover Designer: Keith Plechaty

Created by **Q2AMedia**
Editor: Jessica Cohn
Art Director: Rahul Dhiman
Designers: Harleen Mehta, Tarang Saggar
Photo Researcher: Kamal Kumar
Illustrators: Ashish Tanwar, Indranil Ganguly, Kusum Kala, Nazia Zaidi, Rohit Sharma

Photo credits (t = top; b = bottom; c = center; l = left; r = right):
CDC/Jim Gathany: cover, Christopher Badzioch/Istockphoto: title page, Moodboard/Corbis: 4, Bette Jensen/CDC: 5, Skazka Grez/Shutterstock: 6, Sebastian Kaulitzki/Shutterstock: 7c, Shutterstock: 7b, NIBSC/Science Photo Library: 8, Noam Armonn/Istockphoto: 9, Corbis: 10, Karen Mower/Istockphoto: 11t, Ljupco Smokovski/Istockphoto: 11cr, Tom Le Goff/Digital Vision/Getty Images: 12, Colorized by James Gathany/CDC: 13t, Roger Hutchings/Corbis: 13br, Morgan Lane Photography/Shutterstock: 14t, A.B. Dowsett/Science Photo Library: 14bl, CDC: 14br, Nathalie Speliers Ufermann/Shutterstock: 16t, Dmitrijs Bindemanis/Shutterstock: 16b, Sean Sprague/Alamy: 18-19tl, Tim Boyle/Getty Images: 20, Pakhnyushcha/Shutterstock: 21t, James Gathany/CDC: 21b, Matteo De Stefano/Shutterstock: 22, Hannamariah/Shutterstock: 23tr, Mark Lundborg/Shutterstock: 23b, Donald Gargano/Shutterstock: 24, Simon Fraser/Royal Victoria Infirmary, Newcastle Upon Tyne/Science Photo Library: 25tr, Shutterstock: 25b, Tomasz Trojanowski/Shutterstock: 26, BSIP/Photolibrary: 27t, Fitzwilliam Museum, University of Cambridge, UK/The Bridgeman Art Library: 27b, CDC/World Health Organization: 28, Bettmann/Corbis: 29t, Olga Lis/Shutterstock: 29cr, Bettmann/Corbis: 30t, Michael S. Yamashita/Corbis: 30b, Mary Hilpertshauser/GHO/CDC: 31tr, Crack Palinggi/Reuters: 31b, Eye of Science/Science Photo Library: 32t, CDC: 32b, Sandra Cunningham/Shutterstock: 33, Andrey Kiselev/Fotolia: 34, Xinhua/Xinhua Press/Corbis: 35, Vladimir Melnik/Shutterstock: 36, Julien Tromeur/Shutterstock: 37tr, Alexander Raths/Shutterstock: 38, Ijansempoi/Dreamstime: 39, Bork/Shutterstock: 40bl, Alexander Raths/Shutterstock: 40br, Leah-Anne Thompson/Shutterstock: 41tr, Vladimir Melnik/Shutterstock: 41br, Laurence Gough/Shutterstock: 42, Mika/zefa/Corbis: 43, Darin S. Carroll: 44, Andreas Reh/Istockphoto: 47b
Q2AMedia Art Bank: 9, 15, 17, 18-19,19c, 37b, 40-41, 43bl, 45

All rights reserved. No part of this book may be reproduced, stored in a retrieval system,
or transmitted in any form or by any means, electronic, mechanical, photocopying, recording,
or otherwise, without the prior written permission of the copyright holder. For permission,
contact **permissions@gspub.com**.

Printed in the United States of America
1 2 3 4 5 6 7 8 9 12 11 10 09

CONTENTS

Chapter 1
That's Catchy! 4

Chapter 2
Fighting Germs 6

Chapter 3
Just the Flu? 8

Chapter 4
Tummy Troubles 12

Chapter 5
Bad Bugs 16

Chapter 6
Caught From Critters 22

Chapter 7
Outsmarting Diseases 26

Chapter 8
Exterminators in Action 34

Science at Work 44
Find Out More 45
Glossary 46
Index 48

Words in **boldface** type are defined in the glossary.

Chapter 1

That's CATCHY!

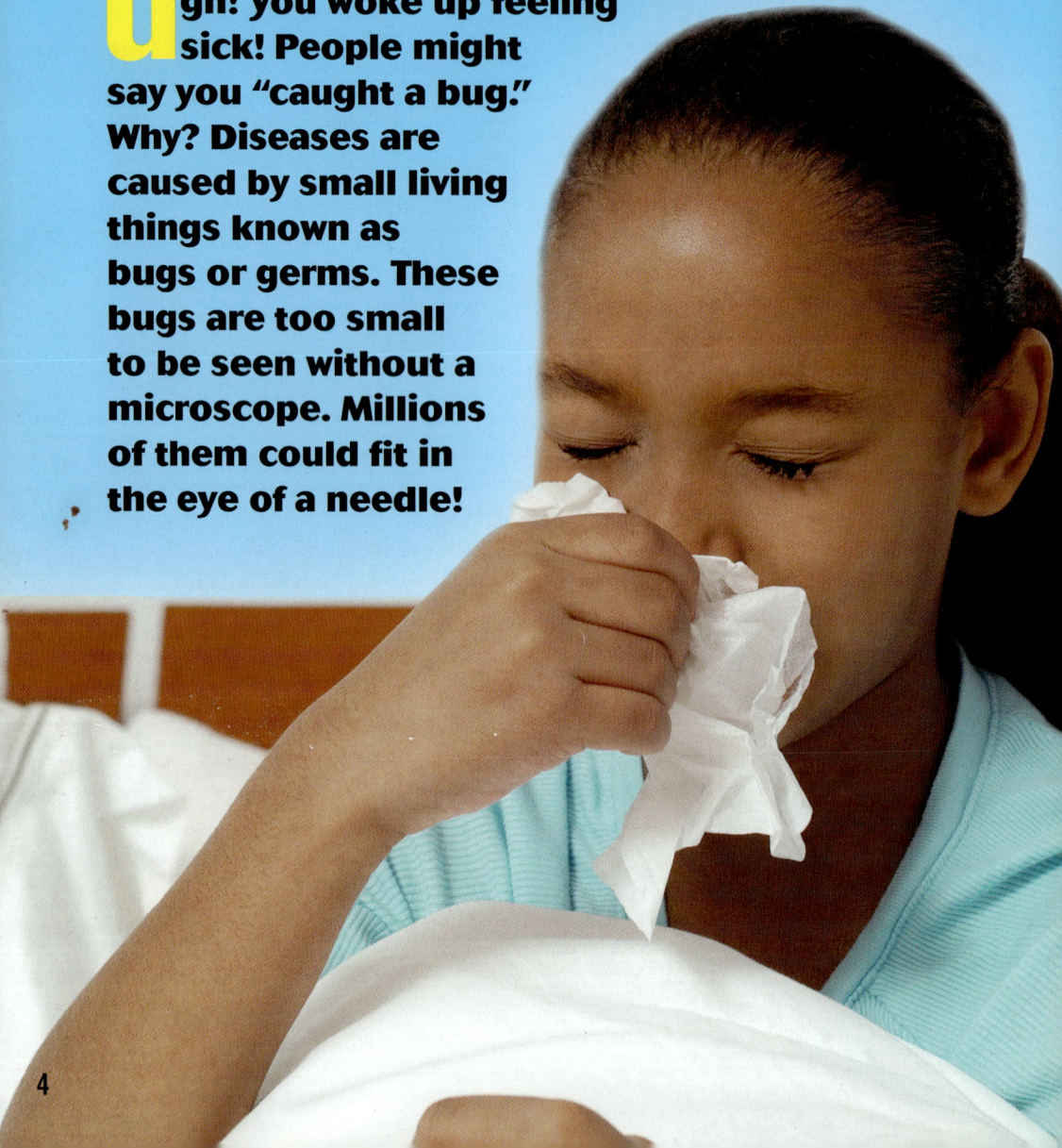

Ugh! You woke up feeling sick! People might say you "caught a bug." Why? Diseases are caused by small living things known as bugs or germs. These bugs are too small to be seen without a microscope. Millions of them could fit in the eye of a needle!

BACTERIA

Scientists call the microscopic germs **microbes**. Microbes include **bacteria**. These tiny living things can cause sicknesses such as strep throat. Not all bacteria cause illness, though. For example, some bacteria help break down the food you eat.

VIRUSES

Viruses are the smallest of microbes that make people sick. They cause illnesses such as colds and measles. Viruses cannot reproduce on their own. They are **parasites**. They must live on or inside another living thing to survive. The organism in which a parasite lives is its **host**.

PROTOZOA

Protozoa are one-celled parasites. They can reproduce but need a host for their babies. Some protozoa enter the body through food or drinking water. Others are spread among people by animals such as insects. Protozoa cause **malaria** and other illnesses.

HOW GERMS SPREAD

Infectious diseases are spread in three ways: person to person, animal to person, and indirect contact. For example, a sick person sneezes into his or her hands and then touches a doorknob. Other people can pick up the germs from the knob.

FAST FACT
Microbes are everywhere. An unwashed hand can have more microbes on it than there are people on Earth!

Tiny bacteria are magnified, or made to look larger, by a microscope.

Chapter 2

Fighting GERMS

One of the best ways to kill microbes is by washing your hands. Wash up before making or eating food. Wash up after coughing, sneezing, and going to the bathroom. Be sure to use soap. Rub your hands together at least 10 seconds. Then rinse away!

FOOD AND FITNESS

Eating healthful food and getting enough exercise keep your **immune system** strong. Make sure that food is fully cooked to kill any microbes. Keep foods at the correct temperature. Some germs are carried in food that has started to spoil, or rot.

VACCINES

Vaccines can help prevent many illnesses. Vaccines contain killed or weakened microbes. They are usually given as a shot. When you get a vaccine, the dead germs enter your body. Your immune system "learns" about the germ. When the system finds that germ in the body again, it "recognizes" the germ and kills it.

The Amazing Immune System

Your body has its own army to fight off microbes. That army is your immune system. The immune system is made up of special **cells** and **organs** that help protect you. Cells are the basic units that make up a living thing. An organ is a body part with certain functions. For instance, your heart is an organ that pumps blood.

Some cells can hunt down bacteria, viruses, and protozoa to kill them. Other cells keep a record of microbes you have fought. If the same kind of microbe invades your body again, these cells alert the killer cells—fast! A fever is a signal that your immune system is fighting a microbe.

Vaccines work with the body's immune system to prevent disease.

7

Chapter 3

Just the FLU?

A flu virus up close

The flu is a common infectious disease. It is caused by a virus. A virus can disguise itself by changing its coating. The body's immune system has a hard time recognizing and fighting the virus.

SIGNS OF THE FLU

People infected with the **influenza**, or flu, virus often have a higher-than-normal temperature. The rise in body temperature is called a fever. Other **symptoms** include chills, headache, and body aches. These symptoms usually last about a week.

Anyone, of any age, can get the flu. In most people, the immune system can fight off the flu. The symptoms go away, and the people feel better. The flu can be more serious in older people and babies, however. It can also be dangerous for people who have other health problems, such as heart disease.

SPREADING FLU

The flu is usually spread through coughing and sneezing. People also touch objects that an infected person has touched. The flu virus can briefly live on those objects. The virus spreads easily, especially in crowded places. The flu survives better outside the body in cold, dry weather. Most people get the flu in winter.

Someone with the flu can spread the illness even before symptoms show up. The sick person remains **contagious** for about seven days after being infected.

A fever can result as the body fights the flu virus.

The Spanish Flu Pandemic of 1918

In 1918 and 1919, a global influenza outbreak killed more than 40 million people. A large disease outbreak is called a **pandemic**. The Spanish flu pandemic was different from other flu outbreaks. The disease affected mostly healthy young adults. Doctors were helpless to stop the spread.

Worldwide, the Spanish flu killed about 50 million people.

Today, scientists track the number of flu cases. It is difficult to know when the next flu pandemic might start. Still, tracking helps doctors detect pandemics early and stop them from spreading.

Flu patients were kept in influenza wards during the Spanish flu pandemic.

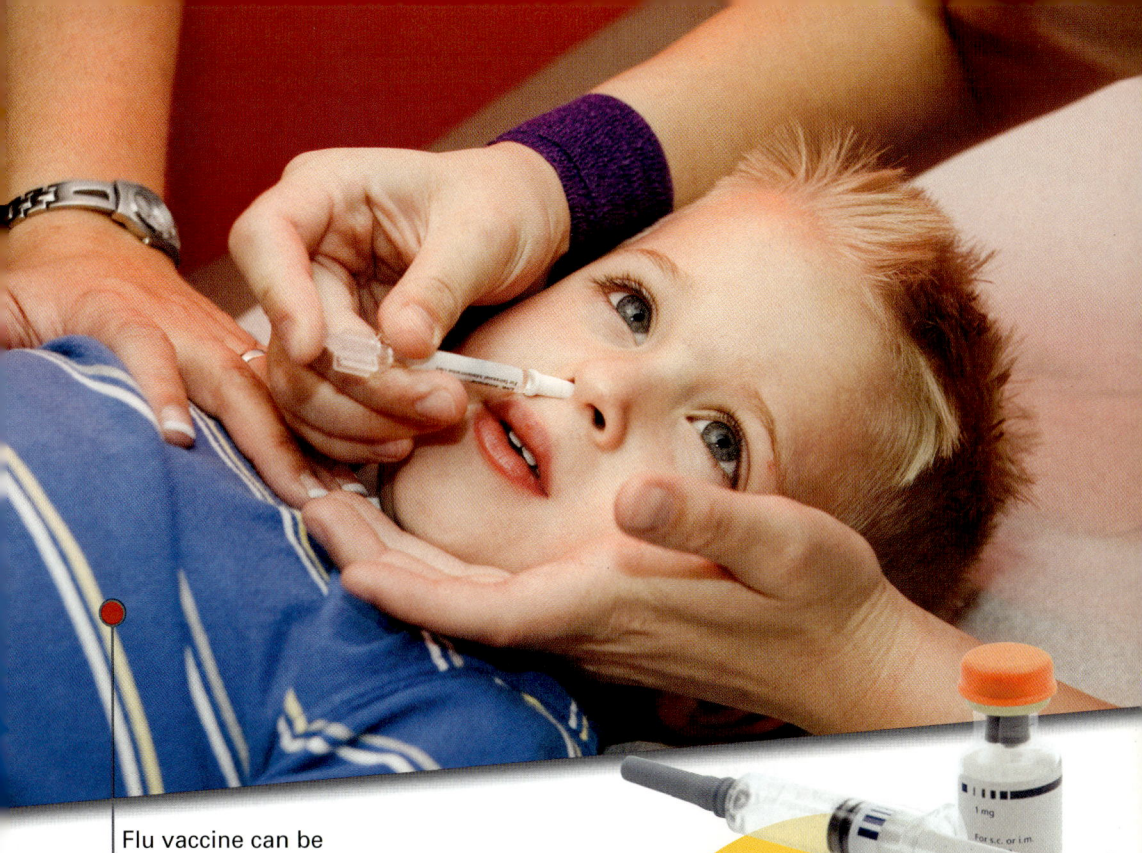

Flu vaccine can be given in a nose spray.

FOILING THE FLU

Doctors recommend that a person with the flu get plenty of rest and drink lots of liquids. The body's immune system fights off the virus. The patient feels better in about a week.

Some patients have additional health problems that make them less able to fight disease. For them, a doctor may prescribe medicine. A few drugs that fight viruses are available. These drugs are different from those that fight bacteria.

The best solution is to avoid getting sick from the start! To protect people, scientists have developed flu vaccines. Because a flu virus can change its outer coating easily, one vaccine does not protect against every type of flu. So scientists make a new flu vaccine every year. They base the ingredients on the types of viruses reported that year. The vaccine can be given in shots or in a nose spray.

WHAT DO YOU THINK?

In some years, there are not enough flu vaccines to go around. Who should get the vaccines first? Why?

11

Chapter 4

Tummy TROUBLES

Some diseases bring tummy troubles. They can be caused by viruses, bacteria, or parasites. The germs are spread through food, unclean water, and body waste.

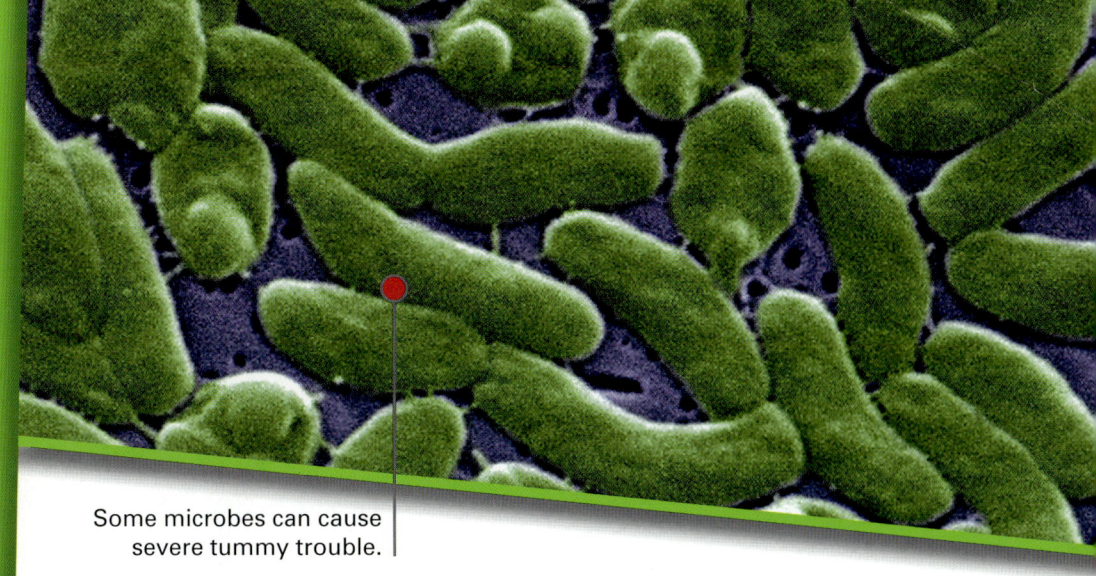

Some microbes can cause severe tummy trouble.

IN THE WATER

Worldwide, many young children die from fluid loss caused by **gastrointestinal (GI)** diseases. These illnesses affect the stomach and **intestines**. People with GI illnesses may throw up. They may also have **diarrhea**.

More than 45 different microbes can cause GI diseases. Most microbes that cause GI problems are spread through water that contains human or animal waste.

GI infections can also spread when people accidentally touch **feces** that contain harmful microbes. A single baby diaper can have more than 100 billion viruses in it! Disease can spread if caretakers do not wash their hands carefully.

PREVENTION IN YOUR HANDS

Currently, doctors do not have vaccines for most gastrointestinal diseases. One of the best methods of controlling these diseases is at your fingertips—hand washing! Communities can also make sure that drinking water does not come into contact with human or animal waste.

Worldwide, many people lack clean drinking water.

Cook eggs and meat thoroughly. Wash fresh foods well.

FOOD FIGHT

Some GI diseases spread when harmful microbes live on or in food. For example, *Salmonella* bacteria live on raw poultry and in uncooked eggs. Cooking poultry and eggs kills the bacteria. The microbes can hang around on surfaces in the kitchen, however. Cutting boards and other items used in preparing raw chicken or turkey should not be reused. Once the items are washed in hot water, you can safely use them again.

E. coli bacteria can also cause illness. These bacteria are common in human and animal feces. *E. coli* can spread when people eat undercooked meat, especially ground beef. Swimming in or drinking unclean water spreads the bacteria, too. Infection with certain types of *E. coli* can cause bloody diarrhea. That condition can be deadly in young children and elderly people.

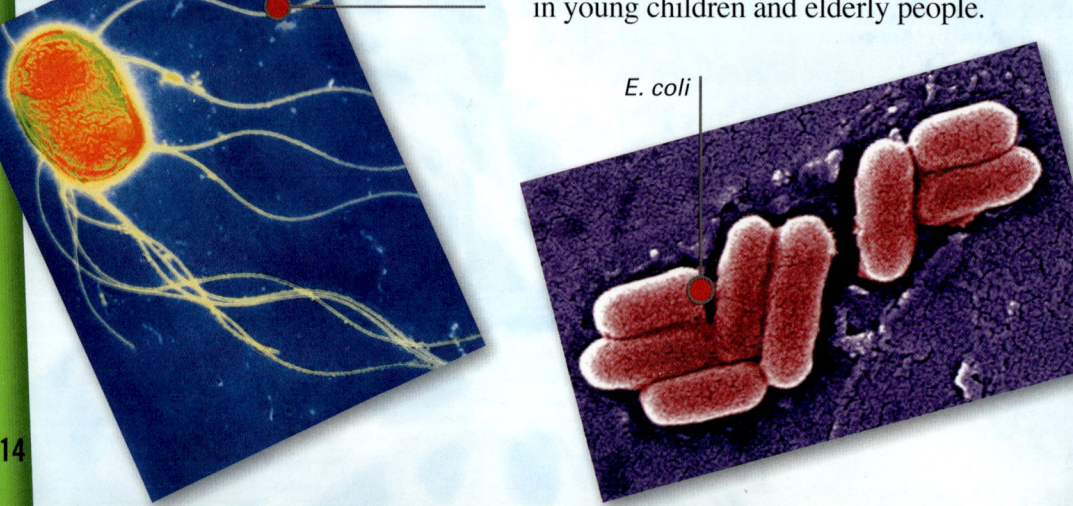

Salmonella

E. coli

YOU DO IT!

Germy Spuds

Caution: Have an adult assist you.

What You Need
- potato
- three plastic storage bags
- marker
- knife

What You Do

Step 1
Mark each bag with a label: CONTROL, UNWASHED, and WASHED. Then have your adult helper wash his or her hands, cut the potato into three parts, and place one part in the bag labeled CONTROL.

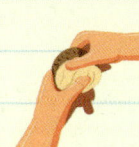  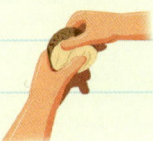 

Step 2
Touch a second potato slice all over with your unwashed hands. Place this slice into the bag marked UNWASHED.

Step 3
Wash your hands thoroughly with soap and water. (Tip: Sing "Happy Birthday" to make sure you wash long enough.) Pick up the last potato slice and touch it all over. Place this slice into the bag marked WASHED.

Step 4
Place the potato slices in a warm, dark place for about a week. At the end of that time, observe each potato slice.

What Happened?
The potato slices in the CONTROL and WASHED bags should look the same. The slice in the UNWASHED bag, however, should look as though it is covered in furry patches. These patches are germs from your unwashed hands. They are growing on the potato!

Chapter 5

Bad BUGS

Microbes are very tiny "bugs" that can cause illness. Insects are bigger bugs that make people sick, too. Some mosquitoes, for instance, carry microbes that cause dangerous diseases.

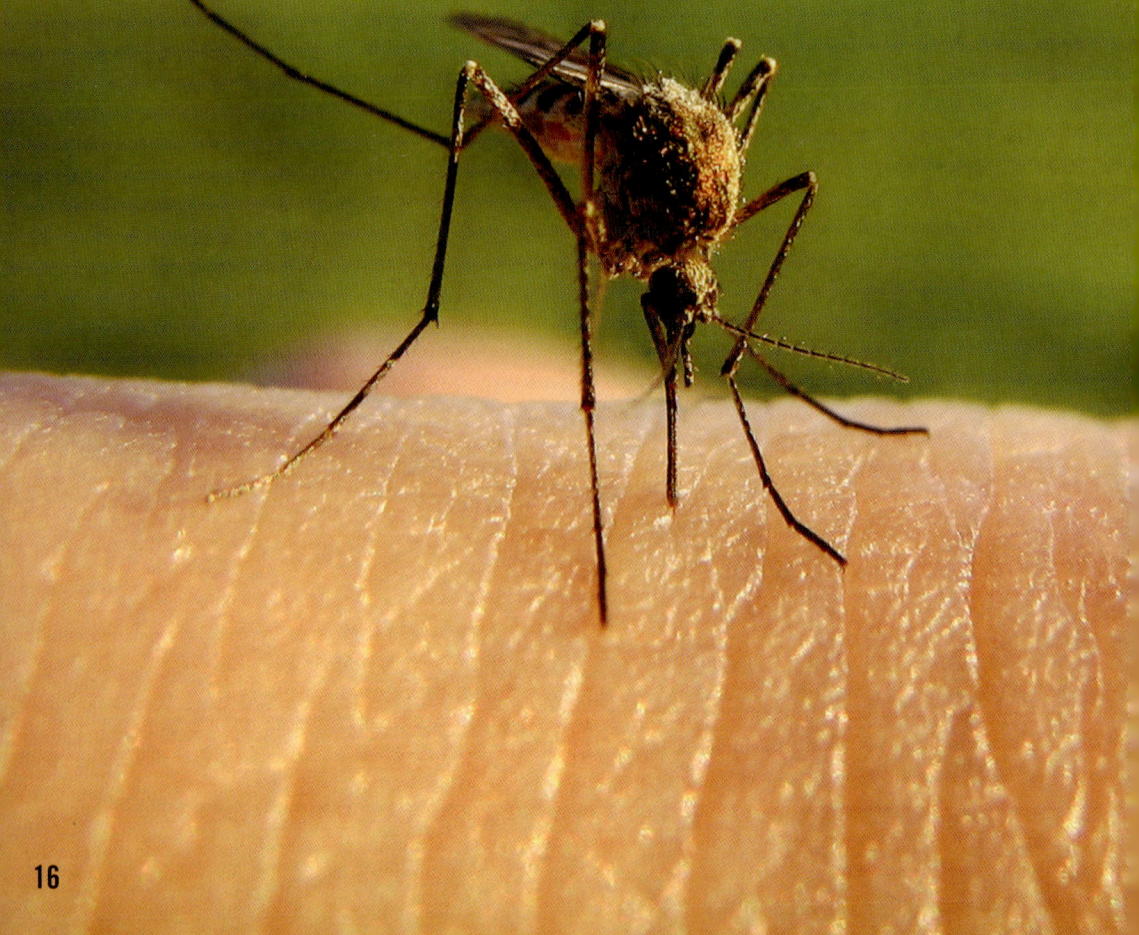

STRAIGHT TO THE CELLS

Malaria is an illness caused by parasites. The parasites pass from person to person. How? A certain type of mosquito sucks a bit of blood from someone with malaria. Then the mosquito bites someone else. The insect injects infected saliva, or spit, into the second person. The parasite then enters the bloodstream.

About 10 to 15 days after the bite, the person may experience headache, fever, vomiting, or extreme tiredness.

FAST FACT
Each year, more than 350 million people get malaria. About 1 million of them die from the disease.

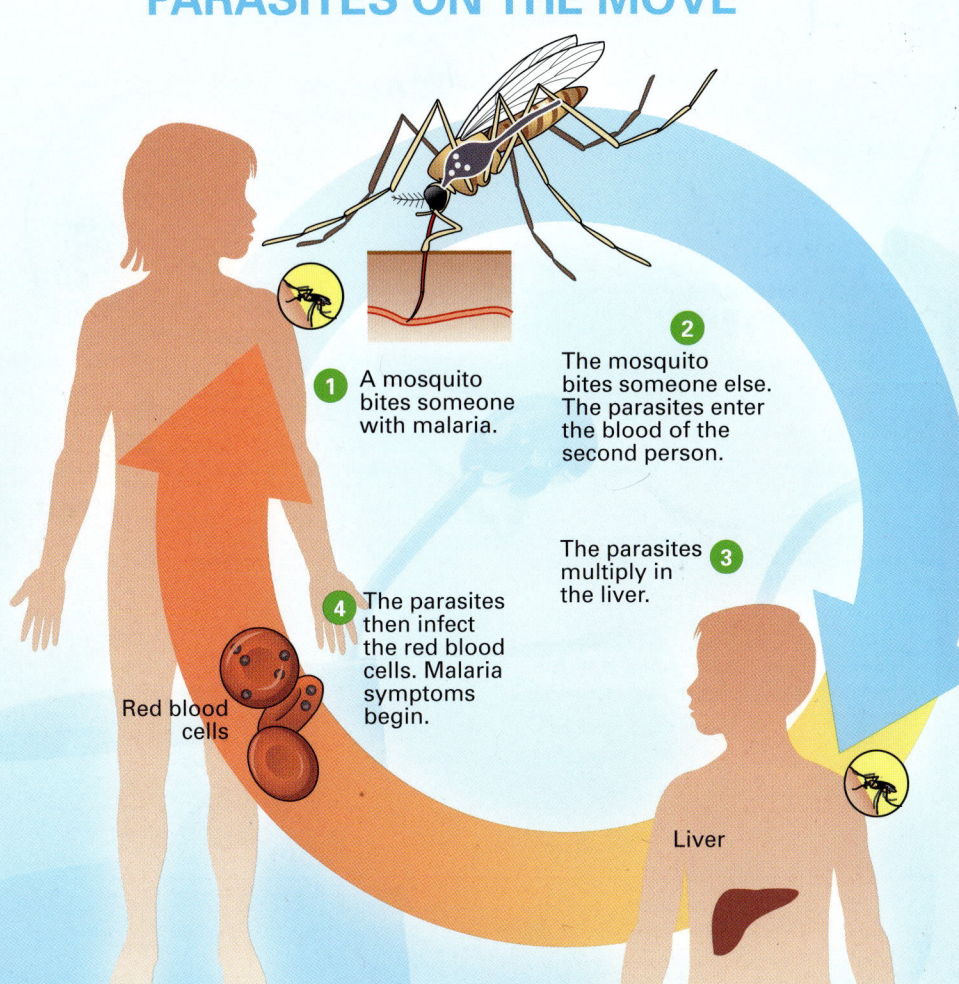

PARASITES ON THE MOVE

1. A mosquito bites someone with malaria.
2. The mosquito bites someone else. The parasites enter the blood of the second person.
3. The parasites multiply in the liver.
4. The parasites then infect the red blood cells. Malaria symptoms begin.

Red blood cells

Liver

17

EXTERMINATING MALARIA

Malaria can be prevented and cured. A vaccine is being developed. If someone is infected, the right medicines can kill the parasite. The medicines need to be taken exactly as the doctor directs.

If malaria is not treated, it can be deadly. The parasites kill red blood cells. The body's organs, such as the brain and the heart, cannot live without the oxygen that red blood cells supply. If a major organ fails, a person can die.

WHO IS AT RISK?

Anyone can get malaria. Most cases, though, occur in warm regions of the world. Malaria is very rare in the United States. The disease is a huge problem in tropical places, though. There, mosquitoes are active year-round. People are bitten more often.

Many people in tropical countries are poor. So the people with the highest risk of infection do not have the best access to the right medications.

MAPPING MALARIA

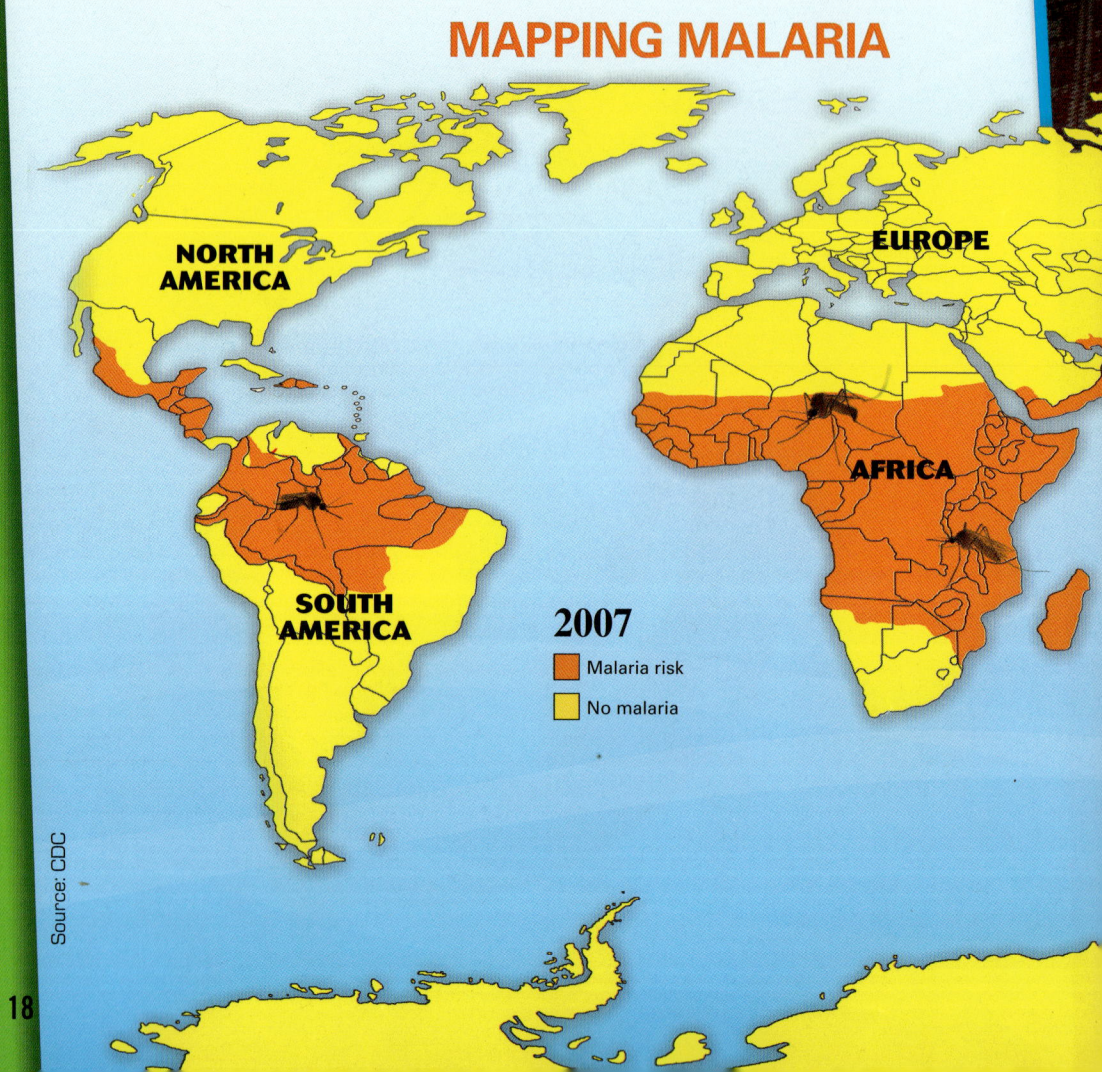

2007
- Malaria risk
- No malaria

Source: CDC

Mosquito nets are helping to cut the number of malaria cases.

STAYING SAFE

How can people avoid being bitten by mosquitoes? They can use insect **repellent**. They can also wear long pants and long-sleeved shirts. Mosquitoes are most active at dawn and dusk. Staying inside during those times lowers the risk of mosquito bites. In places where malaria is a problem, people can spray for insects and sleep under mosquito nets.

Strange but True

Human malaria is transmitted only by females of one type of mosquito. Female mosquitoes need blood so that they can reproduce.

The red bump from a mosquito bite is the body's reaction to mosquito spit. The saliva has a chemical that keeps blood from clumping. That lets the mosquito drink its fill!

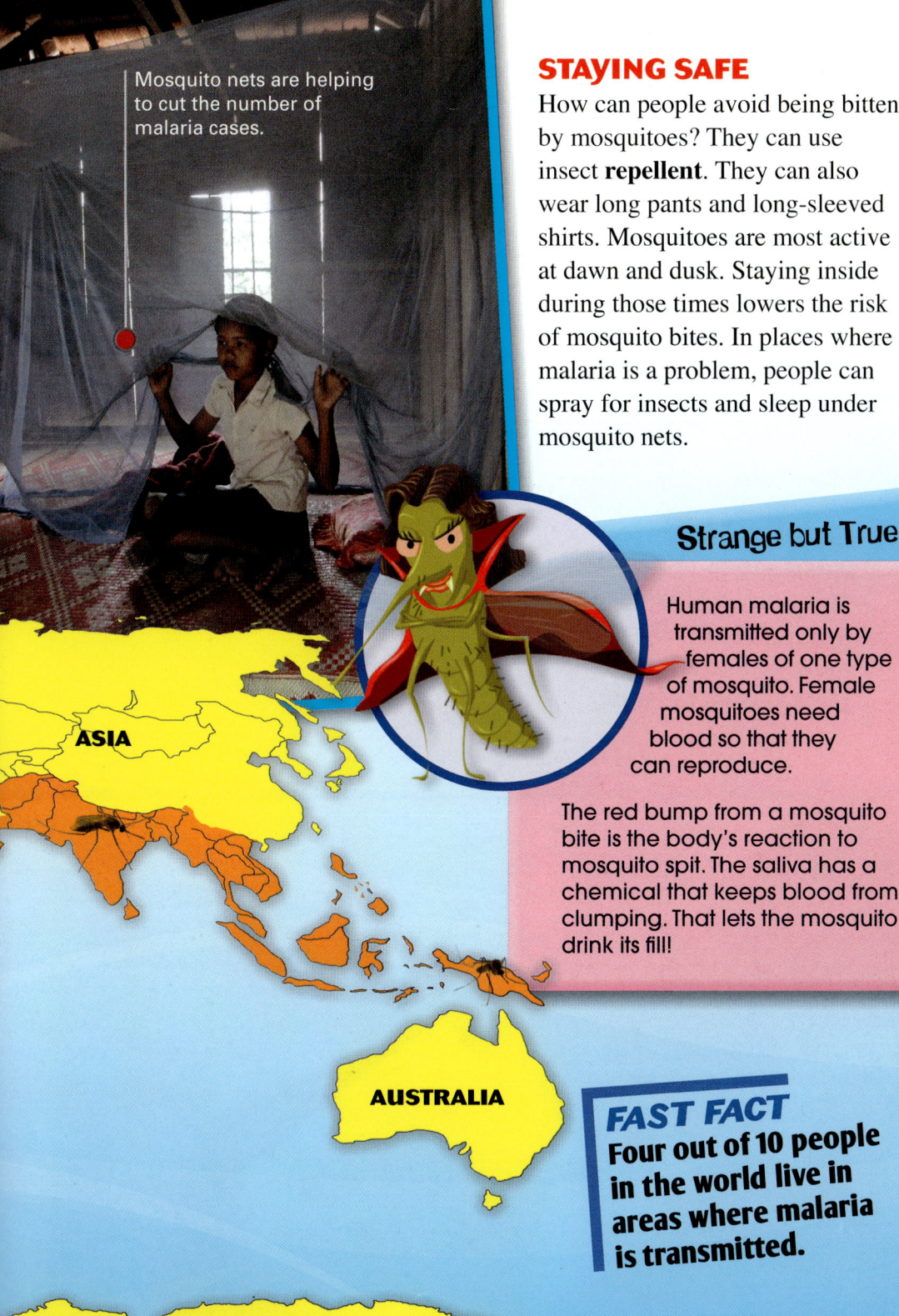

ASIA

AUSTRALIA

ANTARCTICA

FAST FACT
Four out of 10 people in the world live in areas where malaria is transmitted.

WEST NILE VIRUS

Malaria is not the only infectious disease that mosquitoes carry. The mosquito-borne illness **West Nile fever** is more common in the United States. West Nile virus causes West Nile fever. The first human cases of West Nile infection in the United States occurred in 1999. Since then, West Nile virus has been reported in all states except Maine, Alaska, and Hawaii.

> **FAST FACT**
> Mosquitoes like heat. They move slowly at temperatures below 60 degrees Fahrenheit (16 degrees Celsius).

Many animals carry West Nile virus. Most often, the virus spreads to people when a mosquito bites an infected bird and then a person. About 8 in 10 people do not know they were infected because they have very mild symptoms. The unlucky few feel as though they have the flu. Symptoms begin three days to two weeks after a mosquito bite. They may include fever, headache, tiredness, and body aches. In a very small number of cases, severe West Nile disease develops. Vision loss, muscle weakness, or even **paralysis** can occur.

Scientists test mosquitoes for West Nile virus.

LYME DISEASE

Lyme disease is carried by a **tick** and caused by bacteria. Ticks are tiny woodland creatures often mistaken for a kind of insect. They carry bacteria that can cause Lyme disease. The disease spreads when an infected tick bites someone. Then the bacteria get into the person's bloodstream. Lyme disease has flu-like symptoms. Most people also get a **rash** that usually looks like a bull's-eye.

Antibiotics can treat the illness. To avoid the disease, avoid ticks. Stay away from high grass or wooded areas. Wear insect repellent when outdoors. Wear long pants and socks, too. Check for ticks before going back indoors.

Strange but True

A disease called Black Death killed more than one-fourth of the people in Europe in the 1300s. Doctors say Black Death may have been **bubonic plague**. Fleas carried the plague bacteria after biting infected animals, such as rats and squirrels. Then the fleas bit people. Many people think the plague is a thing of the past. But each year, 1,000 to 3,000 people still get it. Modern antibiotics are given to treat the disease.

The Lyme disease rash looks like a target.

Chapter 6

CAUGHT FROM CRITTERS

Animals of all kinds carry disease. Knowing how animals carry disease can help you stay well. You can learn how to handle pets and avoid animals in the wild.

FOR THE BIRDS

Some birds carry viruses that cause a disease called **avian influenza**, or bird flu. From the end of 2003 to the end of 2008, almost 400 people in 14 countries were infected. Scientists are watching bird flu carefully. Doctors want to make sure the viruses do not change to a form that easily spreads to people.

MONKEY BUSINESS

Monkeypox is a rare disease that can spread from animals to people. Scientists first noticed monkeypox in lab monkeys. The virus was later found in squirrels, rabbits, and other animals. Monkeypox is mainly a problem in Africa. In 2003, however, some people in the United States got monkeypox from pet prairie dogs. Humans can get monkeypox by touching or being bitten by an infected animal.

PANDEMIC FEARS

In spring 2009, a new flu virus spread to more than 30 countries around the world. Most cases were mild—like a regular seasonal flu.

Protecting Pets

Even pets can carry disease! Cat scratch fever is caused by bacteria. It usually spreads through a cat scratch or a bite. Symptoms are fever, headache, and tiredness.

Rabies is more serious. This deadly virus usually infects wild animals such as raccoons, skunks, and bats. Dogs and cats can become infected and pass rabies to people through a bite or scratch.

So get your pet vaccinated and keep it away from wild animals. Don't touch wild or stray animals, and don't bring them home.

Prairie dogs can spread monkeypox to people.

In Mexico, though, more than 50 people died from the new flu. The virus is a mix of avian, swine, and human flu viruses. It spreads from human to human through coughing, sneezing, or touching objects with flu viruses on them.

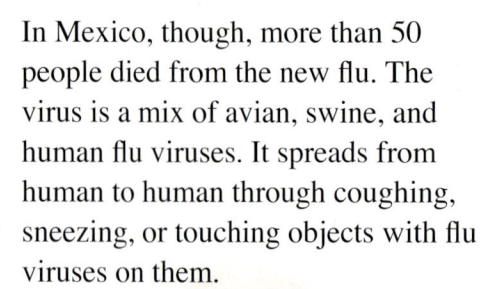

BAD NEWS EBOLA

It sounds like a horror movie. People bleed from their eyes, mouth, nose, and ears. Within weeks, their organs fail. They die. How did they get the killer disease? By eating infected animals!

The **Ebola virus** sickens gorillas, chimpanzees, and humans. In 2005, researchers found that some fruit bats carried the virus. The virus may have passed to people who ate the bats. People and animals can also spread it through blood or body fluids.

The disease usually begins with flu-like symptoms. Diarrhea, vomiting, a rash, and bleeding can follow. The disease usually ends in death. Most cases have occurred in countries in

Gorillas have died from the Ebola virus.

FAST FACT
The Ebola virus was named for a river in Zaire, Africa. The virus was discovered there in 1976.

Africa. Scientists are working to make a vaccine to protect people against the Ebola virus.

SICK COWS

Cows can get a deadly illness called **mad cow disease**. The illness affects a cow's **nervous system**, causing the animal to act strangely. The brains of infected animals are full of holes. They look like sponges!

Doctors say people can get a similar disease by eating meat from an animal with mad cow disease. No cases have been reported in the United States. The disease currently has no treatment or cure.

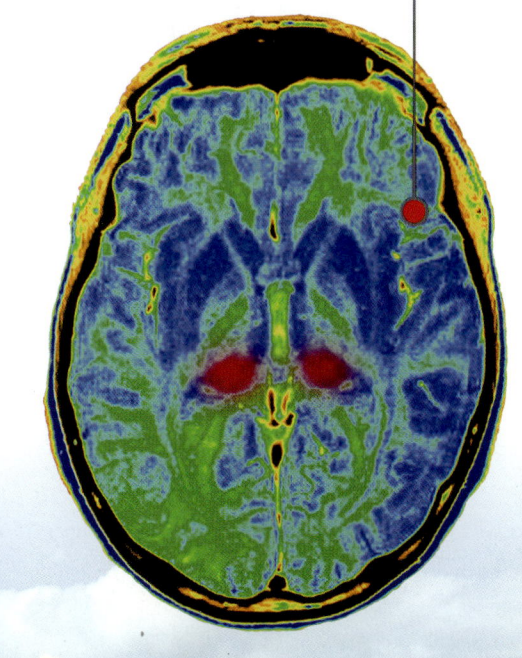

Brain scans of people with the human form of mad cow disease show a certain pattern.

Cows are tested for mad cow disease in some countries.

25

Chapter 7

Outsmarting DISEASES

Are you feeling surrounded by sickness? Don't fear! Every day, doctors and scientists look for ways to outsmart sneaky microbes. Researchers have already succeeded in the fight against several diseases.

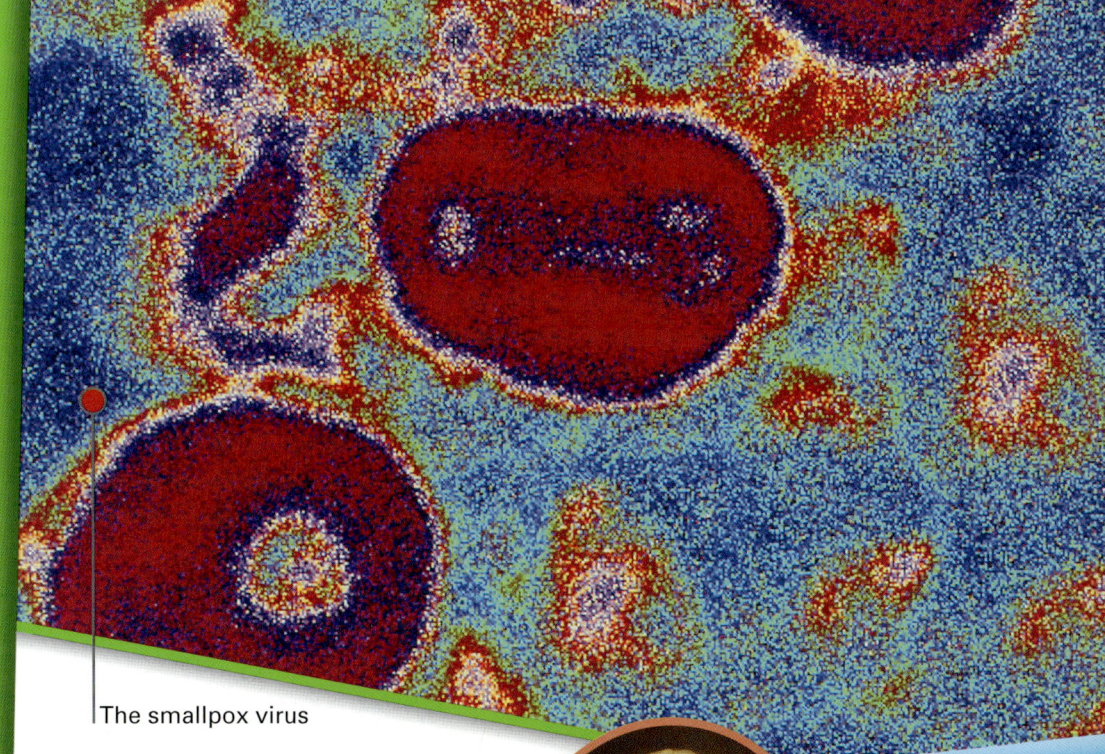

The smallpox virus

THE SMALLPOX STORY

Smallpox begins with flu-like symptoms. Then a rash of raised bumps shows up. The blisters become crusty, scab over, and fall off. Smallpox looks like chicken pox but makes people much sicker.

The virus spreads from person to person through coughing or sneezing. Contact with infected bedding can also spread the virus. Only humans carry the virus. Animals and insects cannot.

In the past, smallpox killed about one-third of the people who became infected. Many of them were infants and young children. People who recovered, however, never got the disease again. That fact helped doctors outsmart smallpox!

Strange but True

George Washington, the first U.S. president, survived malaria, smallpox, and **tuberculosis (TB)**. TB is a disease that affects the lungs. All three diseases are serious.

When the president died, he had a sore throat. Historians believe the sore throat was caused by a bacterial infection. They also believe he died from the treatment rather than the illness. Why? Doctors used to drain blood from sick people. Doctors thought that getting rid of "bad" blood would help speed recovery.

SUCCESS!

In the 10th century, doctors in China and India purposely infected people with a mild form of smallpox virus. The doctors took liquid from the blisters of people who had a mild case of the disease. Then the doctors put the liquid under the skin of healthy people. Sometimes it worked! A lucky person would get a mild case of smallpox. He or she was protected from the serious form for life. The method was not completely safe, though. Some people died. In 1796, an English doctor named Edward Jenner developed a vaccine that worked without killing people. A worldwide vaccination program wiped out the virus. The last case of smallpox in the United States was reported in 1949. The last case in the world was reported in Somalia in 1977.

After the smallpox virus was wiped out, doctors stopped vaccinating people against the virus. The U.S. government keeps enough vaccine for every American, though. Officials want to be ready if the virus shows up again.

WHAT DO YOU THINK?
Which disease will doctors and scientists exterminate next?

Ali Maow Maalin was the last known person to get smallpox.

Edward Jenner, Medical Pioneer

The answer to the smallpox vaccine came to Edward Jenner in 1796. A milkmaid (a woman who milks cows) named Sarah Nelmes came to see Jenner. She had a case of **cowpox**, a skin disease. Cowpox is similar to smallpox but milder. Jenner knew that people with cowpox did not catch smallpox during an outbreak in 1788. He knew there was a connection.

Jenner took some of the liquid from Sarah's sores. He also got some liquid from the blisters of a patient with mild smallpox. Jenner made two small cuts in the arm of a boy named James Phipps. The doctor put the fluid from Sarah's cowpox blisters into the cuts. James came down with a mild case of cowpox and quickly got better. Six weeks later, Jenner did the same thing with the smallpox virus.

The idea worked! James stayed well. Jenner called his method vaccination, from the Latin word *vaca*, or "cow." By 1800, almost all doctors were using Jenner's method.

U.S. President
Franklin D. Roosevelt
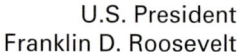

FAST FACT
President Franklin Delano Roosevelt was infected with the polio virus in 1921. The virus left the president in a wheelchair. He wore metal braces on his legs to help him walk.

GOOD-BYE, POLIO
A disease called **polio** can rob people of their ability to walk. In 1952, almost 60,000 Americans were infected with the polio virus. More than 3,000 of them died. Today, however, scientists are closer to wiping out the disease worldwide. The virus was exterminated in the United States by 1979.

Doctors are still working to wipe out polio in some parts of the world.

VALUABLE VACCINES

In 1955, a polio vaccine developed by Jonas Salk became widely available. The Salk vaccine contains dead polio viruses that "train" the immune system. It is given as a shot. In 1957, Albert Sabin developed a second vaccine. Sabin's vaccine can be taken by mouth. Today, both types of vaccines are used to protect children around the world.

Polio still exists in some places, though. In 2008, the largest polio outbreaks were in Afghanistan, India, Nigeria, and Pakistan. Doctors are trying to make sure every child gets vaccinated. They hope to wipe out the disease worldwide. They are making progress. In 1988, about 350,000 polio cases were reported. By the end of 2006, the number had dropped to fewer than 2,000.

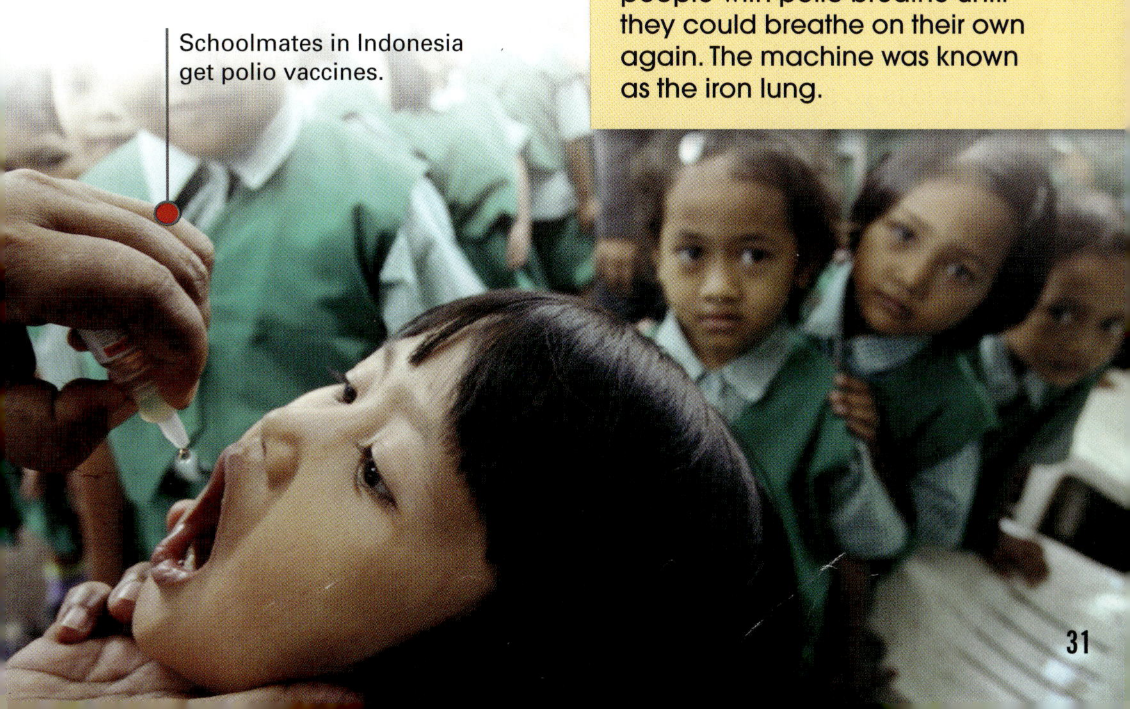

Schoolmates in Indonesia get polio vaccines.

The Iron Lung

The symptoms of polio range from mild flu-like symptoms to paralysis. Polio sometimes results in death. The polio virus can attack the nervous system and leave muscles unable to work. If the paralysis affects a person's legs, he or she can no longer walk. If the paralysis affects the muscles used for breathing, the person cannot breathe.

In 1927, Philip Drinker and Louis Agassiz Shaw developed a special machine. It helped people with polio breathe until they could breathe on their own again. The machine was known as the iron lung.

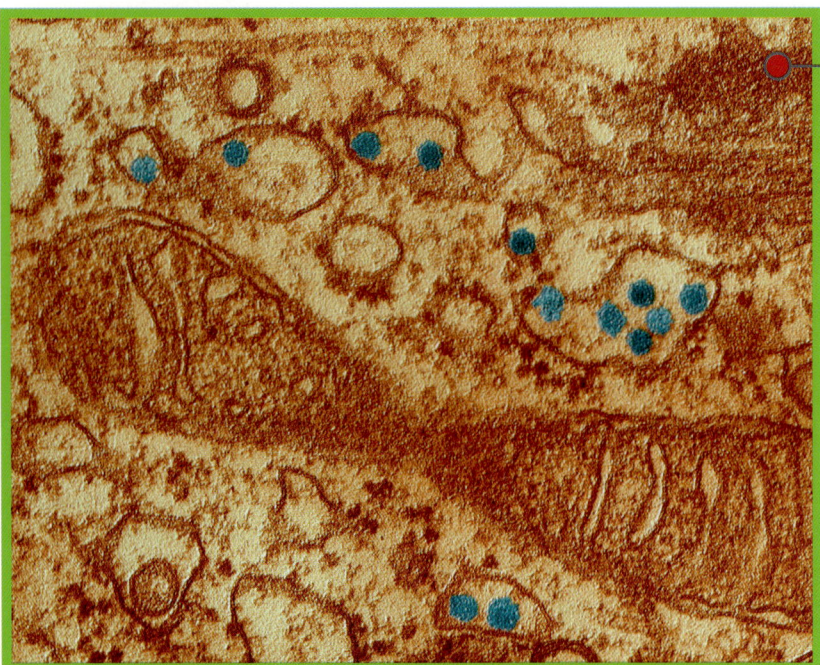

The rubella virus

CHILDHOOD ILLNESS

Another important vaccine protects young children from **measles**, **mumps**, and **rubella**. It is known as the MMR vaccine. The vaccine contains weakened forms of all three viruses. Most children in the United States get this vaccine before they are allowed to go to school.

Measles causes flu-like symptoms and a rash. Rubella, or German measles, causes similar symptoms. Measles is rare in the United States but kills many people in some places, such as Africa. The virus spreads when infected people cough or sneeze. People who are not vaccinated can get sick from breathing the germs.

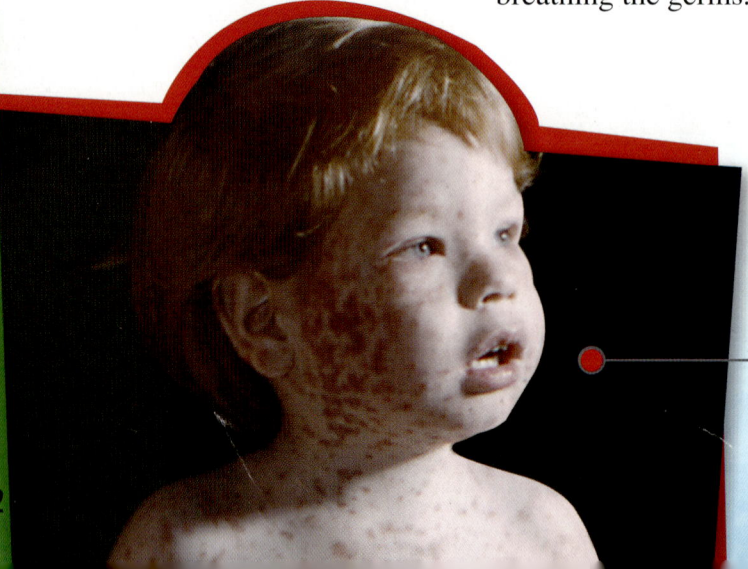

The measles rash starts on the face, neck, and forehead. It appears on the body, arms, and legs next.

The virus that causes mumps infects **glands** on the sides of the face. The glands swell (puff up) and hurt. The swelling makes the sick person look like a chipmunk with food stored in its cheeks! The mumps virus spreads through coughing and sneezing, too.

Doctors are trying to make sure that all children are vaccinated against measles, mumps, and rubella. These diseases may then become a thing of the past.

Measles Menace

Measles and mumps are rare in the United States. In 2006, however, mumps sickened 3,200 people in 12 states. Most of the sick people were teenagers or young adults in the Midwest. Two years later, 131 cases of measles were reported in the United States. Scientists found that most of those people had probably not been vaccinated. Because measles is very contagious, it can quickly reappear when vaccination rates go down.

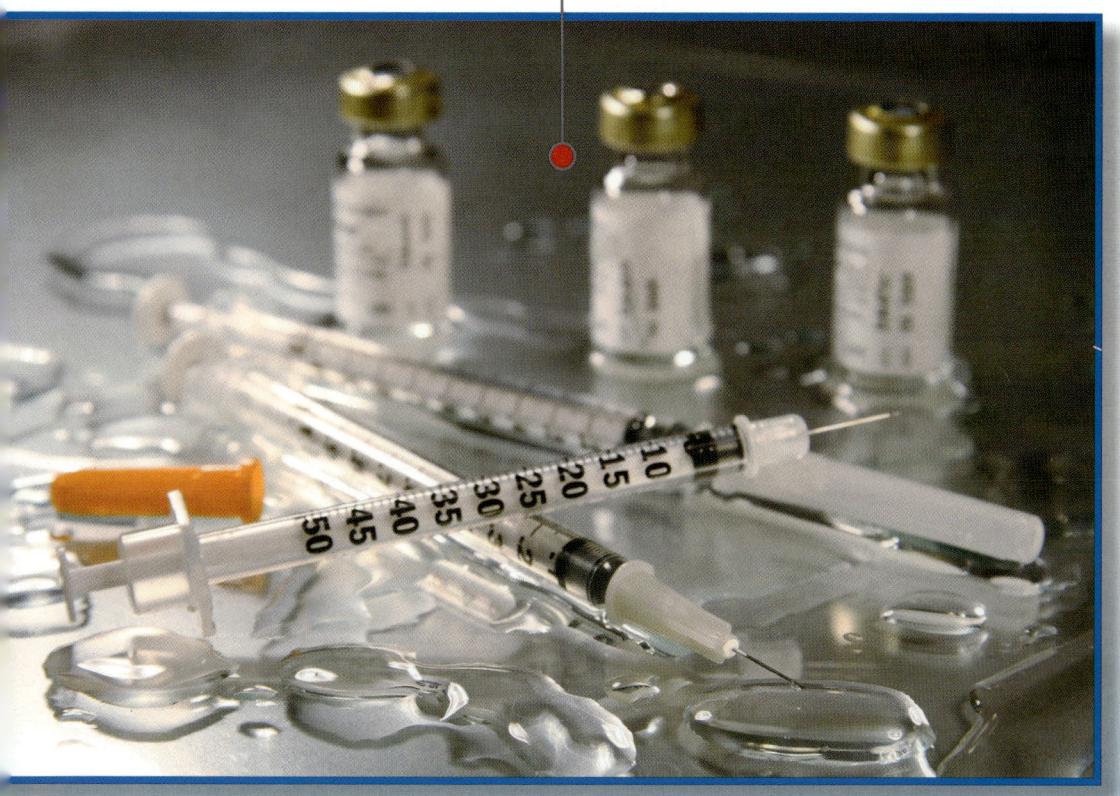

One shot protects kids against measles, mumps, and rubella.

Chapter 8

Exterminators in Action

A huge number of people are working to wipe out the world's worst diseases. Some researchers track the path of disease. Other exterminators look for cures. Some people help by raising money for medicine and research.

Students in China use handprints to paint a red ribbon. The design is known as the AIDS ribbon.

A GLOBAL CHALLENGE

The disease **AIDS** was first recognized in the United States in 1981. Scientists soon discovered that a virus known as **HIV** causes AIDS. HIV weakens the body's immune system.

Doctors say HIV has been around a long time. They are still unsure where the virus started. It may be related to a virus that causes a similar disease in African monkeys.

Today, doctors give patients medicines that can help fight off infections related to HIV and AIDS. The medications are very expensive. Worldwide, 33 million people are infected with HIV. About 30 million of them live in poor countries. Experts estimate that at least 10 million infected people in poor countries do not get the costly medicines they need.

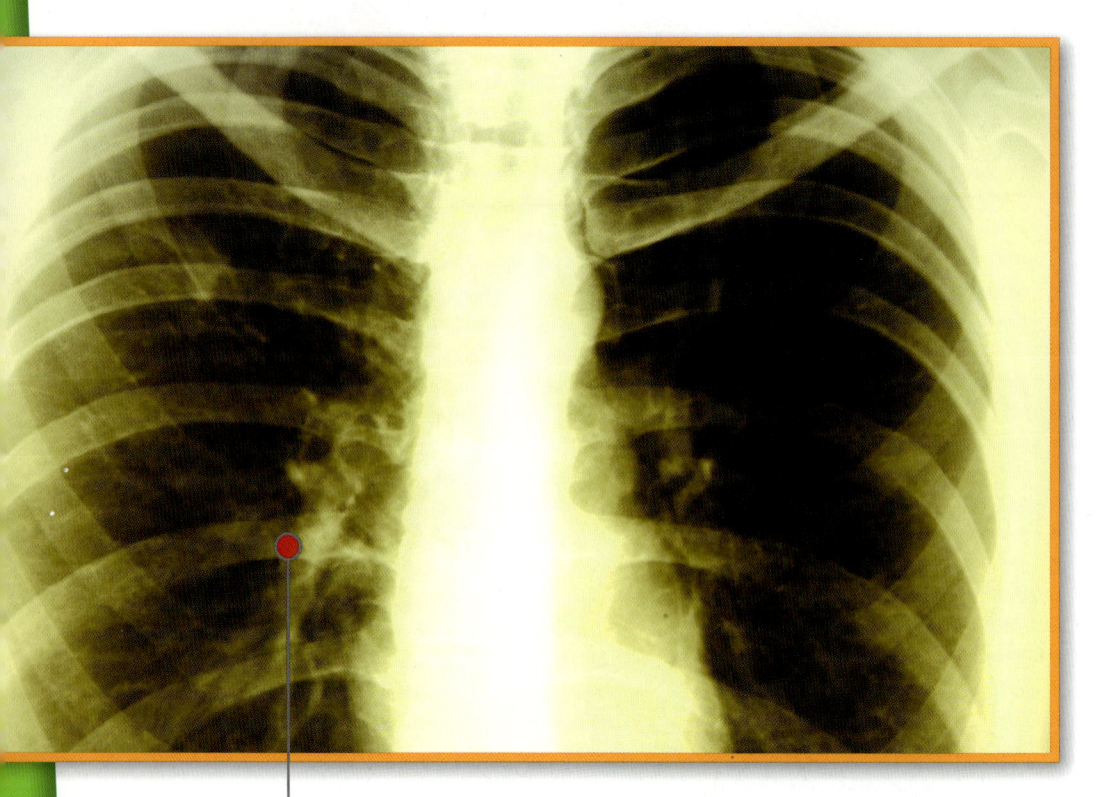

Tuberculosis mainly affects the lungs.

HELP AT HOME AND BEYOND

Many of the scientists who protect people from infectious diseases work for the Centers for Disease Control (CDC) or the World Health Organization (WHO). The CDC is an agency of the U.S. government. It monitors disease outbreaks within the United States. The agency was formed in the 1950s, during the fight to wipe out malaria in the United States. Scientists at the CDC also do research. They try to find new ways to beat infectious diseases. The WHO is an agency of the United Nations. The WHO does similar work all over the world.

SUPERBUGS ATTACK!

Sometimes, diseases that scientists thought they had under control appear again. The microbes that cause them may be even stronger than before. For example, a new kind of tuberculosis does not respond to the drugs commonly used to treat that disease. Tuberculosis is caused by bacteria that attack the lungs. Some of those bacteria have become "superbugs." The usual drugs do not kill them.

Another superbug in the news is **MRSA**. It is a nasty skin infection caused by **staph** bacteria. First, sores appear on the skin. The disease can spread inside the body and cause great damage. MRSA is tough to treat because it resists antibiotics.

Scientists say superbugs develop partly because people misuse medicines. People with bacterial illnesses do not always take antibiotics as their doctors prescribe. For example, sometimes people stop an antibiotic when their symptoms go away. Not all of the bacteria are killed, though. The ones that remain—and multiply—are better able to resist the drug. These people may get sick again. They then need a stronger antibiotic to get better.

Drugs for Bugs?

Another problem is the use of antibiotics to treat colds and flu. Those illnesses are not caused by bacteria. They are caused by viruses. Antibiotics do not work against viruses. Instead of treating the disease, antibiotics are more likely to kill helpful bacteria inside the body. Then resistant bacteria grow and multiply.

Steps to Stop MRSA

1. Wash your hands. If you cannot wash with soap and water, use a sanitizer.

2. Cover cuts, even small ones, with bandages.

3. Do not touch anyone's wounds or bandages.

4. Do not share personal items, such as towels.

5. Shower after exercising. Wash towels in hot water.

37

Researchers at health agencies track disease outbreaks.

MICROBES ON THE MOVE

Malaria is showing up in new areas. Some scientists say a global rise in average temperatures is partly to blame. The scientists believe that Earth's warming is making some places warmer and wetter. That change enlarges the area where mosquitoes can live. More people are exposed to mosquitoes—and the diseases they carry.

The ease of travel today also exposes more people to more diseases. For example, malaria has not been a problem in the United States since the 1950s. Yet more than 1,300 people who live in the United States get the disease each year. Almost all of those people are exposed to the malaria parasite while visiting countries where the disease is still a problem.

Researchers at the CDC and the WHO track disease in humans and in animals. They record disease outbreaks on a map. This method helps doctors and scientists decide where medicines are needed. Tracking also helps prevent larger outbreaks of disease.

WHAT DO YOU THINK?

Are diseases easier or harder to fight today than they were in the past? Why?

People travel more than ever. The germs that cause disease go with them!

CS INFOGRAPHIC

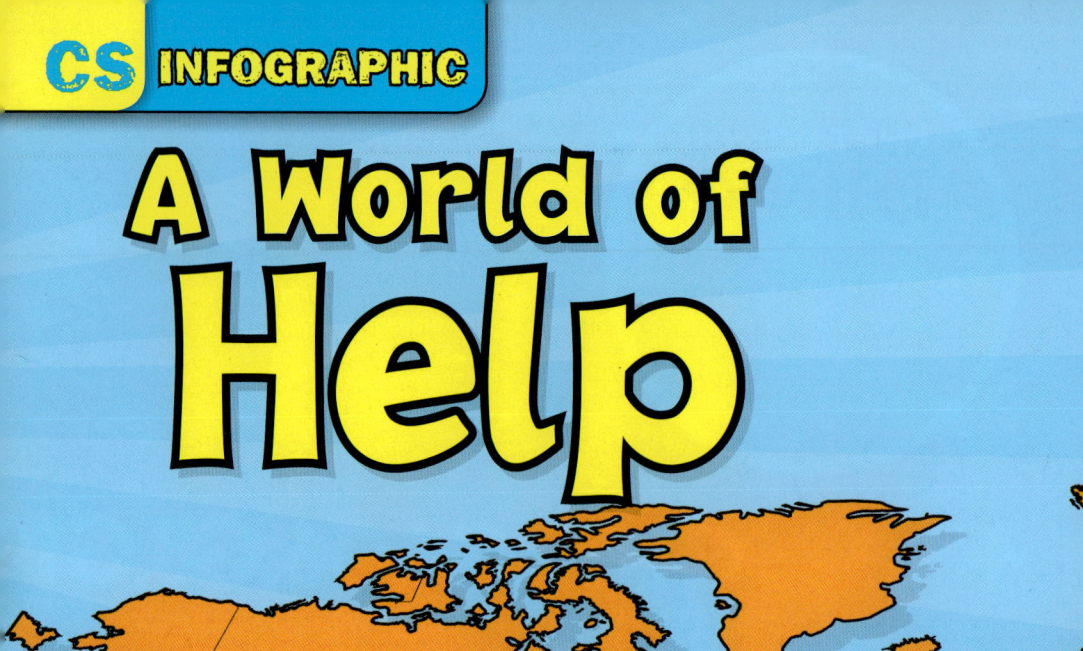

A World of Help

NORTH AMERICA

SOUTH AMERICA

AFRICA

Researchers in Baltimore, Maryland, have found a way to spot the malaria parasite in urine. The urine dipstick will help doctors **diagnose** malaria more quickly and easily.

Scientists in Manchester, England, are developing new types of antibiotics to fight powerful superbugs. These bacteria are resistant to other antibiotics.

Many scientists are working on ways to combat infectious diseases. Here is a look at some current research.

The WHO is based in Geneva, Switzerland. WHO researchers track the types of flu viruses that make people sick each year. The researchers use that information to help develop that year's flu vaccine.

EUROPE

ASIA

AUSTRALIA

Researchers from several countries are working together to protect all people from tuberculosis. The group has developed a TB vaccine. The scientists are testing the vaccine in South Africa and the Philippines.

ANTARCTICA

WINNING OUT

Researchers around the world are developing new ways to diagnose, treat, and prevent infectious diseases. Scientists at the National Institutes of Health (NIH), for example, are studying the 1918 flu pandemic. They want to find out how the flu spread and why some people survived. By learning more about this historic outbreak, they hope to better protect people from future pandemics.

Researchers do important work in labs throughout the world.

Other scientists at the NIH are studying how mice respond to a bird flu virus. The researchers are taking immune cells from people who survived bird flu. The researchers hope their work leads to a vaccine.

Many scientists are working on medicines that will fight superbugs. Some researchers are testing a drug to fight the new form of TB. Still others are searching for a cure for HIV and AIDS. Maybe someday these science superheroes will conquer infectious diseases.

A doctor treats a sick child in Ghana. Will today's research bring a disease-free future?

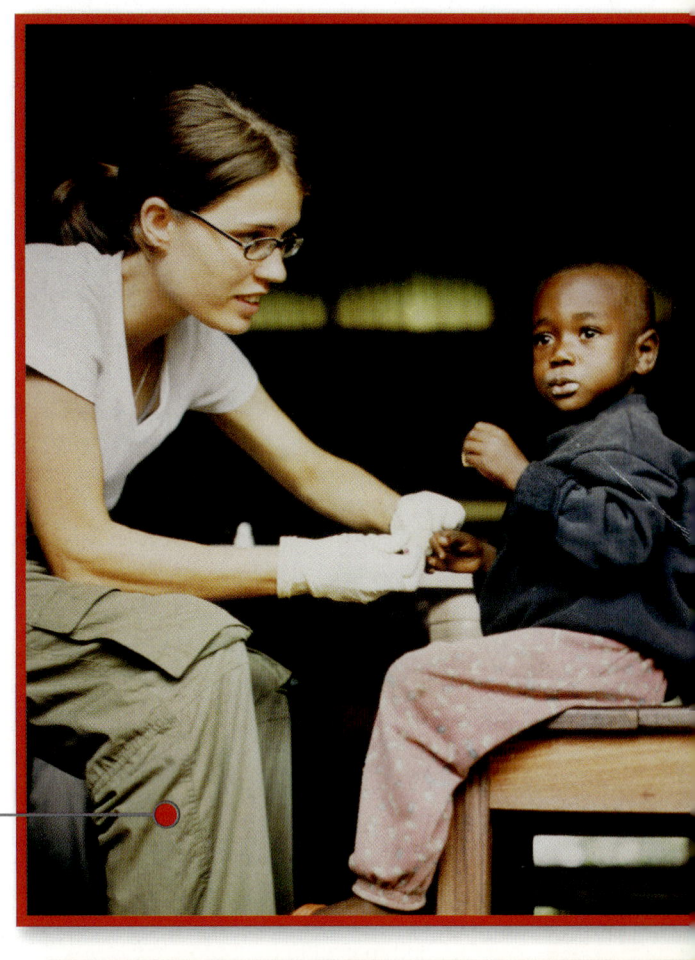

How You Can Help

You can help fight infectious diseases, too. Here are just a few ways.

- Wash your hands often, but especially after going to the bathroom and before eating.
- Use medicines exactly the way your doctor tells you—every time.
- Do not approach or touch wild animals.
- Make sure food is cooked all the way through before you eat it.

SCIENCE AT WORK

MEDICAL SCIENTIST

Job Description: Medical scientists study human diseases, including infectious ones, to try to find new ways to diagnose, treat, and prevent them.

Job Outlook: Employment is expected to increase.

Earnings: $35,490 to $117,520, with most medical scientists earning about $61,680.

Source: Bureau of Labor Statistics

Conversation With an Infectious Disease Specialist

Darin S. Carroll, Ph.D., is a specialist in infectious disease at the Centers for Disease Control and Prevention. He has traveled to the Congo and Ghana to study infectious diseases.

HOW DID YOU CHOOSE THIS JOB?

I got interested in science because I liked learning about animals and nature. During my third year of college, there was an outbreak of [a form of severe **pneumonia**]. It was carried by a kind of deer mouse. That got me interested in studying **zoonotic** diseases [diseases carried by animals].

WHAT IS THE BEST PART OF YOUR WORK?

Learning things that will help prevent people from getting sick!

WHAT IS YOUR TYPICAL DAY LIKE?

There really is no "typical" day at CDC. Usual days in the office are spent reading papers and reports. Usual days in the field are spent finding out how many people are sick, where they are, and how they became infected. I also make recommendations on how to help prevent other cases. It is often hard to know what exactly you will be doing each day.

HOW CAN INTERESTED PEOPLE PREPARE FOR A JOB IN MEDICAL SCIENCE?

Read! I remember that I was always drawn to books or magazine articles, even some TV shows, about animals and nature. Find that area of science that draws you in, and learn all you can about it. Once you start learning enough to begin asking questions, then you have taken the first step toward becoming a scientist.

FIND OUT MORE

BOOKS

Emmer, Rick. *Virus Hunter.* New York: Chelsea House Publishers, 2006.

Herbst, Judith. *Germ Theory.* Minneapolis: Lerner Publishing Group, 2007.

Hirschmann, Kris. *The Ebola Virus.* San Diego: Lucent Books, 2006.

Snedden, Robert. *Fighting Infectious Diseases.* Chicago: Heinemann, 2007.

WEB SITES

CDC Rabies for Kids Page
www.cdc.gov/ncidod/dvrd/kidsrabies
Know the facts about preventing rabies.

KidsHealth for Kids
www.kidshealth.org/kid
Nemours offers health information on many topics.

The Why Files: Mosquito Bytes
www.whyfiles.org/016skeeter/index.html
Learn about mosquitoes and more.

Publisher's note to educators and parents: Our editors have carefully reviewed these web sites to ensure that they are suitable for children. Many web sites change frequently, however, and we cannot guarantee that a site's future contents will continue to meet our high standards of quality and educational value. Be advised that children should be closely supervised whenever they access the Internet.

GLOSSARY

AIDS (acquired immune deficiency syndrome): a weakened condition of human cells

antibiotics: medicines that can kill bacteria

avian influenza (bird flu): a type of viral disease in birds

bacteria: single-celled microbes that can sometimes cause infections

bubonic plague: a serious bacterial disease that swells the body

cells: small, complex units in plants and animals

contagious: easily spread from one person to another

cowpox: a type of viral disease in cows

diagnose: to identify what is causing an illness

diarrhea: frequent, runny feces

Ebola virus: a group of related, serious viral diseases

feces: solid waste that is eliminated from the body

gastrointestinal (GI): affecting the stomach and intestines

glands: organs that produce certain substances

HIV (human immunodeficiency virus): virus-related agents leading to AIDS

host: an organism a parasite lives in or on

immune system: a system of special cells and organs that protects the body from disease-causing microbes

infectious: having microbes that cause disease

influenza (flu): a viral disease that causes fever, coughing, and body aches

intestines: lower sections of the body canal through which food passes

Lyme disease: a bacterial illness spread by ticks

mad cow disease: a brain disease in cows

malaria: a disease of the blood, spread by mosquitoes

measles: a disease that causes red spots on skin

microbes: microscopic living things

MRSA: a type of bacteria that is resistant to drugs

mumps: a viral disease that causes glands in the neck to swell

nervous system: cells and tissues of brain, nerves, and related body centers

organs: body parts adapted for special jobs

pandemic: a sudden, widespread outbreak of disease

paralysis: the loss of the ability to move a body part

parasites: organisms that live on or in another organism

pneumonia: an infection of the lungs

polio: a viral disease of the spinal cord

protozoa: single-celled organisms that can divide only within a host

rabies: a viral disease of the nervous system

rash: an outbreak of redness or spots on the skin

repellent: a substance that keeps away insects

rubella: a viral disease similar to measles

smallpox: a serious viral disease with fever and rash

staph: the short name for bacteria that can infect body tissues

symptoms: signs of disease

tick: a tiny animal that attaches to human or animal skin to feed on blood

tuberculosis (TB): a bacterial disease of body tissues, especially of the lungs

vaccines: medicines that "train" the immune system to "recognize" a microbe

viruses: tiny microbes that live inside other organisms and cause disease

West Nile fever: a disease that passes from birds to mosquitoes to people

zoonotic: spread by an animal

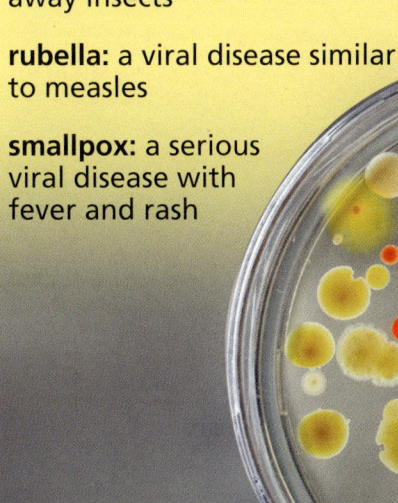

INDEX

AIDS 35
antibiotics 21, 36, 37, 40
avian influenza 23, 42

bacteria 5, 7, 11, 12, 14, 21, 23, 27, 36, 37, 40
bubonic plague 21

cells 7
Centers for Disease Control (CDC) 36, 38, 44
contagious 9, 33
cowpox 29

diagnose 40, 42
diarrhea 13, 14, 24
Drinker, Philip 31

Ebola virus 24
E. coli 14

feces 13, 14
flu 8-11, 21, 24, 27, 31, 32, 41, 42

gastrointestinal (GI) 13, 14
germs 4, 12, 15, 39
glands 33

HIV 35
host 5

immune system 7, 8, 10, 11
infectious 5, 8, 20, 42-44
influenza See flu.
intestines 13
iron lung 31

Jenner, Edward 28, 29

Lyme disease 21

Maalin, Ali Maow 28
mad cow disease 25
malaria 5, 17-19, 20, 27, 36, 38, 40
measles 32, 33
microbes 5-7, 13, 14, 16, 26, 36, 38
monkeypox 23
mumps 32, 33

National Institutes of Health (NIH) 42, 42
Nelmes, Sarah 21
nervous system 25, 31

organs 7, 18, 24

pandemic 10, 42
paralysis 20, 31
parasites 5, 12, 17, 18, 40
Phipps, James 29
pneumonia 44

polio 30, 31
protozoa 5, 7

rabies 23
rash 21, 24
repellent 19
Roosevelt, Franklin D. 30
rubella 32, 33

Sabin, Albert 31
saliva 17, 19
Salk, Jonas 31
Salmonella 14
Shaw, Louis Agassiz 31
smallpox 27, 28
superbugs 36, 37, 40
symptoms 9, 20, 23, 32

tick 21
tuberculosis 27, 36, 40, 43

vaccinate 23, 31, 33
vaccines 7, 11, 18, 24, 28, 29, 31, 32, 41, 43
virus 5, 7-9, 11-13, 23, 24, 27-30, 32, 33, 35, 37

West Nile fever 20
World Health Organization (WHO) 36, 38, 41

zoonotic diseases 44

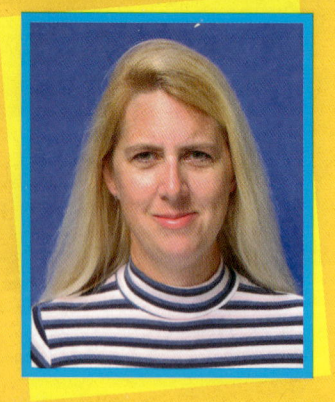

About the Author

Kristi Lew is the author of more than two dozen science books for teachers and young people. Before becoming a full-time writer, she worked in laboratories for more than 10 years and taught high-school science. When Kristi is not writing, she enjoys sailing with her husband on their boat, *Proton*. She writes, lives, and sails in St. Petersburg, Florida.